PRESENTED TO:

FROM:

DATE:

Redeemer

nicole c. mullen

NASHVILLE, TENNESSEE

www.jcountryman.com

Design: AndersonThomas Design, Inc., Nashville, Tennessee
Project editor: Kathy Baker

ISBN 0-8499-5753-2

Printed and bound in the United States of America

www.thomasnelson.com

Oh, give thanks to the LORD, *for He is good!*
For His mercy endures forever.
Let the redeemed of the LORD *say so,*
Whom He has redeemed from
the hand of the enemy,
And gathered out of the lands,
From the east and from the west,
From the north and from the south.

PSALM 107:1-3

A Note from Nicole

*C*ertain stories in the Bible have always been my favorites, Ruth is definitely one of those, and so is Job. They're both stories about the powerful redemption of people who had it all, lost everything, then found blessing on the other side of pain.

Job is extremely relevant to people these days, and when I talk about this story every night at my concerts, I get so many comments afterward. People identify with Job because they're going through things. They think: Here I am living a normal life, I'm a good citizen, love the Lord, do what I think is right, then all of a sudden I find myself stricken with cancer, my son is taken away from me, and my finances are gone. These things hit from left and right, people don't have a clue as to why. They're like "what happened?" "What did I do wrong?" And those are the questions that Job asked: "What did I do wrong? Show me my faults so that I can get it right." Sometimes we're not given those kinds of answers; we don't understand the whole scheme of things at the time.

And to me, the story of Ruth and Naomi is a lot like that, too. The book of Ruth is not so much about Ruth as it is about Naomi. She becomes the female Job to me. Like him, Naomi has it all, then she loses it. For a while she's thinking nothing good will happen to her, but later in the story the people are saying, "Blessed be *Naomi*. God has shown her mercy, and God has sent her a kinsman-redeemer." Ruth is used as an instrument of God—and she herself receives redemption—but to me the book is more about the female Job.

And of course, these redemption stories are just foretastes of the great Redemption offered by Jesus to all of us.

A Note About the Song

I have always had a fascination with the Cinderella tale—
you know, the rags to riches theory. This idea always has
been borrowed to lend hope to those of us who dream of
being more than our surroundings, economics, or status
would allow. But on one particular day, I found myself
being overtaken by a couple of true *riches to rags* stories.

There I was sitting on the couch, with my burgundy-
colored Bible opened to the book of Job. I read about
all that happened to him and how he was faithful even
through his pain. And then I saw a familiar phrase,
there in my Bible, that jumped out at me in a new way.

"I know that my Redeemer lives" (Job 19:25).

What a statement of faith! Job endures so much—he
even challenges God—but he ends up proclaiming God's
glory. It was the first time I'd really noticed the *context*
of this phrase in the Bible, and the power of it just
spoke to me.

The song "Redeemer" celebrates the power of a God who "laid the foundations of the earth" (Job 38:4) and "shut in the sea with doors" (Job 38:8) but who still loves and redeems *us*.

While I wrote the song, I was struggling with the idea that my problems, compared to Job's problems, didn't amount to anything. Still in the midst of his mountain of troubles, Job was able to proclaim his faith in his Redeemer, and I realized that if Job was able to, then despite anything I had gone through or was going through I should be able to proclaim it, too.

I should be able to hope against hope like Job and cling to the assurance that I know my Redeemer lives. I may not know why, but I know my Redeemer lives. I may not know what's going to happen tomorrow, but I know my Redeemer lives. I may not know how I'm going to pay my rent, but I know my Redeemer lives. Or whatever the issue is, I *know* my Redeemer lives.

REDEEMER

by nicole c. mullen

Who taught the sun where to stand in the morning?
Who told the ocean you can only come this far?
Who showed the moon where to hide 'til evening?
Whose words alone can catch a falling star?

❋ ❋ ❋

Well I know my Redeemer lives
I know my Redeemer lives
All of creation testifies
This life within me cries
I know my Redeemer lives

The very same God that spins things in orbit
Runs to the weary, the worn and the weak
And the same gentle hands that hold me when I'm broken
They conquered death to bring me victory.

❄ ❄ ❄

I know my Redeemer lives
Let all of creation testify
Let this life within me cry
I know my Redeemer, He lives

❄ ❄ ❄

To take away my shame
And He lives forever, I'll proclaim
The payment of my sin
Was the precious life He gave
But now He's alive and
There's an empty grave

Let me tell you about Job. Here we have a man who lives in the land of Uz. He has ten kids—seven boys and three girls. He owns seven thousand sheep, three thousand camels, five hundred yoke of oxen, and five hundred donkeys. He also has a large number of servants. Not to mention enough land and house space for everybody.

Job is declared the greatest man among the people of the East. To top it off, **God calls Job blameless and upright.**

Who taught the sun where to stand in the morning?

Oh, that my words were written!
Oh, that they were inscribed in a book!
That they were engraved on a rock
With an iron pen and lead, forever!
For I know that my Redeemer lives,
And He shall stand at last on the earth;
And after my skin is destroyed, this I know,
That in my flesh I shall see God,
Whom I shall see for myself,
And my eyes shall behold, and not another.
How my heart yearns within me!

JOB 19:23-27

And then comes the drama.

One day the good angels along with the not-so-good angel—the devil—present themselves before God. Job's name comes up, and God boldly declares him to be a man who "fears God and shuns evil" (Job 1:8). The devil replies that Job's loyalty is only because he has been blessed and protected, and he wagers that if the aforementioned are lifted, then Job would surely curse God to His face.

The challenge is accepted. "And the Lord said to Satan, 'Behold, all that he has is in your power; only do not lay a hand on his person' " (Job 1:12).

can only come this far?

So down to earth the devil goes. His mission is to destroy all that Job has. His goal is to get him to curse God.

In the matter of a day, Satan attacks Job's income by wiping out eleven thousand animals, and then he steals the lives of all ten of Job's kids.

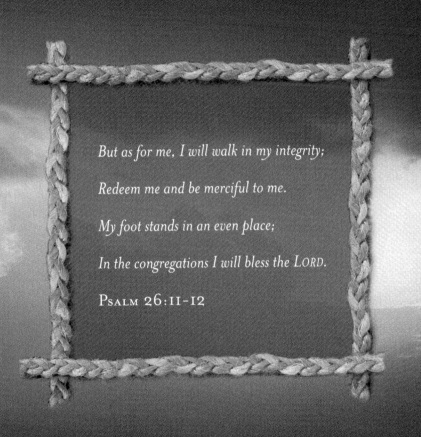

But as for me, I will walk in my integrity;

Redeem me and be merciful to me.

My foot stands in an even place;

In the congregations I will bless the LORD.

PSALM 26:11-12

Now the one who has been declared blameless is faced with a dilemma. Curse God or...

The servants ran back to the house and informed Job of his fate. How could something that was going so well turn so bad so quickly?

> Then Job arose, tore his robe, and shaved his head; and he fell to the ground and worshiped. And he said:

> "Naked I came from my mother's womb,
> And naked shall I return there.
> The Lord gave, and the Lord has taken away;
> Blessed be the name of the Lord."

> In all this Job did not sin nor charge God with wrong (Job 1:20-22).

Who showed the moon
where to hide 'til evening?

Not too thrilled with his defeat, the devil stands before God again and states that the reason Job blessed and not cursed was because his flesh was spared. And so this time the devil is given permission to inflict as much pain as he'd like. The only limitation is to spare Job's life.

It must have been tough being the recipient of such an onslaught. Job has plenty of questions but no answers, and now his body is covered in sores from the top of his head on down to his feet. When he sleeps, he has nightmares. His close friends falsely accuse him of wrongdoing. Even his wife tells him to curse God and die.

Whose words alone can

catch a falling star?

*S*till in the midst of all his pain and suffering, Job holds onto a seed of hope—buried beneath the dirt, the wind and the rain of his circumstance. It begins to sprout. And he says to himself and his friends alike,

"I know that my redeemer lives."

Even when nothing else makes sense, Job has confidence that the One who can save him is alive. And he's right! Job also says, "He shall stand at last upon the earth, and after my skin is destroyed, this I know, that in my flesh I shall see God" (Job 19:25–26).

What faith!

Job eventually is restored. The Lord makes him prosperous and gives him twice as much as he had before the calamities. He also has ten more children, his last days are better than the first, and he lives a long, full life.

*I know that
my Redeemer lives*

Our God is a redeeming God!

Job, despite all his confusion and misery, knows this and trusts Him. The women Naomi and Ruth also lose everything and then are redeemed. We don't hear of a challenge in the heavens over them, but we do know what happened to them here on earth.

"Thus says the LORD, the King of Israel,

And his Redeemer, the LORD of hosts:

I am the First and I am the Last;

Besides Me there is no God."

Isaiah 44:6

The very same God that
spins things in orbit

26

God loves and cares for each individual person, people like Elimelech and Naomi, who live in the town of Bethlehem. They have two sons, Mahlon and Chilion. When a famine arises in Bethlehem, the family picks up their belongings, says goodbye to friends and moves to Moab—a foreign country with foreign gods.

While they're there, Elimelech dies, leaving Naomi alone with their two sons. With the death of their dad, the sons must get serious about the future of the family name and its property, so they start by getting local wives for themselves. Chilion's wife is Orpah, and Mahlon marries Ruth. Naomi loves these women and there's mutual respect between them. Still I wonder if there's an underlying tension in that every month for about ten years neither bride carries a child in her womb. Do the women feel like they have failed? Do other people accuse them and say "see, I told you those marriages would never work" . . . "that house is cursed with barrenness and death" . . . "at least one of them should have had a son by now to keep and save what is rightfully theirs."

Maybe Naomi comforts her daughters-in-law with the story of Sarah. The matriarch of the Jewish people. She, too, was barren until her old age, and then God worked a miracle. He opened her womb and through her a nation was born. Naomi is alive because of that miracle. What he did for Sarah, He could do for Orpah and Ruth. But for some reason the God of Israel chooses not to grant either woman a son or a daughter.

IS THEIR BARRENNESS A PUNISHMENT, OR DOES HE SIMPLY HAVE ANOTHER PLAN?

And then the unthinkable happens.

Before they can return to the country of their birth or produce a child to carry on the family, Mahlon and Chilion die.

Naomi is now left in a foreign land with no husband, no sons, no hopes of having grandchildren.

She is bitter in spirit.

What will these women do for food? Who will save them from the shame of having to beg? Who will protect and provide for them? What man will accept women who apparently can't have children?

Who will *redeem* them?

*Runs to the weary,
the worn and the weak*

"Do not fear, for you will not be ashamed;
Neither be disgraced, for you will not be put to shame;
For you will forget the shame of your youth,
And will not remember the reproach of your
  widowhood anymore.
For your Maker is your husband,
The LORD of hosts is His name;
And your Redeemer is the Holy One of Israel;
He is called the God of the whole earth.
For the LORD has called you
Like a woman forsaken and grieved in spirit,
Like a youthful wife when you were refused,"
Says your God.
"For a mere moment I have forsaken you,
But with great mercies I will gather you.
With a little wrath I hid My face from you for a moment;
But with everlasting kindness I will have mercy on you,"
Says the LORD, your Redeemer.

ISAIAH 54:4–8

When Naomi hears that "the LORD had visited His people by giving them bread" (Ruth 1:6), she decides to return home. Maybe someone among the children of Israel will have mercy upon a widow who outlived her sons. Once they were packed, the three women set out on the road to the land of Judah.

Before they are far on their way, Naomi stops and urges her daughters-in-law to return home to their people. After much crying and convincing, Orpah agrees to return to her mother's house and to her god. Ruth however clings to Naomi and begs to come with her.

"Entreat me not to leave you,

Or to turn back from following after you;

For wherever you go, I will go; And wherever you lodge, I will lodge;

Your people shall be my people, And your God, my God.

Where you die, I will die, And there will I be buried.

The LORD do so to me, and more also,

If anything but death parts you and me"

RUTH 1:16–17

And so together they journey to Bethlehem, where the whole town is abuzz because of them. Where are Elimelech, Mahlon, and Chilion? What has happened to them? Why does Naomi look so old and depressed? Who is this foreigner with her from Moab? Doesn't she know that we don't want her kind around here?

> And the women said, "Is this Naomi?" But she said to them, "Do not call me Naomi [which means pleasant]; call me Mara [which means bitter], for the Almighty has dealt very bitterly with me. I went out full, and the LORD has brought me home again empty" (Ruth 1:19–20).

Naomi and Ruth need a kinsman-redeemer—a close relative to buy the property of their dead husbands, take in the widows, produce heirs on the men's behalf, and carry on their family. The land and property would not be the possession of the purchaser; rather, it would belong to the son born to him and the wife of the deceased. What kind of a man would do such a thing?

aomi and Ruth find shelter, but they still need food. So Ruth, a woman of character and humility, goes to pick up the left over grain behind the workers during the barley harvest. She finds herself working in a field belonging to a wealthy man named Boaz. He takes notice of Ruth and gives her an open invitation to glean in his field. He promises that she would be safe as she works there.

He also praises her for being gracious to her mother-in-law, and for the sacrifices she had made in leaving her family and coming to live among strangers. At the end of her first day of work, Ruth rushes home to tell Naomi of the favor she had found.

"The LORD bless him!" Naomi said to her daughter-in-law. "He has not stopped showing his kindness to the living and the dead." She added,

"That man is our close relative;
he is one of our kinsman-redeemers."
(Ruth 2:20, NIV)

The same gentle

Naomi encourages Ruth to continue working in the field of Boaz.
And when Naomi tells Ruth how they could be taken care of in the
future, Ruth agrees to do her part. So Ruth bathes, perfumes
herself and puts on her finest clothing. And when it's dark and
quiet on the threshing floor, she finds Boaz among the other men,
goes to him, uncovers his feet, lies down next to them and places
the bottom of his blanket over herself.

hands that hold me...

In the middle of the night, Boaz is startled and he discovers Ruth's presence. She humbly announces herself, and asks if he would spread his garment over her and become the kinsman-redeemer. Boaz is elated. He thanks Ruth for choosing him over anyone else, and he praises her for her character and her reputation.

Early the next day, Boaz goes to the town gate to speak with a closer relative who has first claim to being the kinsman-redeemer. At first he wants to redeem the property, but then declines when he learns he would also have to take Ruth as a wife. Boaz then accepts the responsibility of kinsman-redeemer. That day he purchases the property from Naomi and marries Ruth, the widow of Mahlon. God blesses their union, opens her womb—which had been barren for so many years—and gives them a son, whom they name Obed.

The women said to Naomi: "Praise be to the Lord, who this day has not left you without a kinsman-redeemer. May he become famous throughout Israel! He will renew your life and sustain you in your old age. For your daughter-in-law, who loves you and who is better to you than seven sons, has given him birth" (Ruth 4:14–15, NIV).

Conquered death to bring me victory.

In time, Obed becomes the father of Jesse, and Jesse fathers David, the shepherd boy who becomes king. And many generations later, in this same family, in this same town of Bethlehem, is born the

REDEEMER OF REDEEMERS, JESUS THE CHRIST.

But the angel answered and said to the women, "Do not be afraid, for I know that you seek Jesus who was crucified. He is not here; for He is risen, as He said. Come, see the place where the Lord lay. And go quickly and tell His disciples that He is risen from the dead, and indeed He is going before you into Galilee; there you will see Him. Behold, I have told you."

MATTHEW 28:5–7

The God who thundered His power before Job and rescued two poor widows is the same God who humbled Himself and became one of us. From eternity past 'til the moment of His conception, He had dwelt in unapproachable light.

At any given moment He could summon legions of angels to wait upon Him and do His bidding. He was constantly worshiped and adored. His surroundings, which He made for Himself, were beautiful beyond description.

I know my redeemer lives
All of creation testifies
This life within me cries
I know my redeemer lives

Then, in order to redeem His fallen creation—
His people made in His image—

He became one of us.

Born in a smelly stable, feeling the cold air upon
His bare skin for the first time, the small Savior
was wrapped in the swaddling cloth of death as a
reminder of His mission in this life.

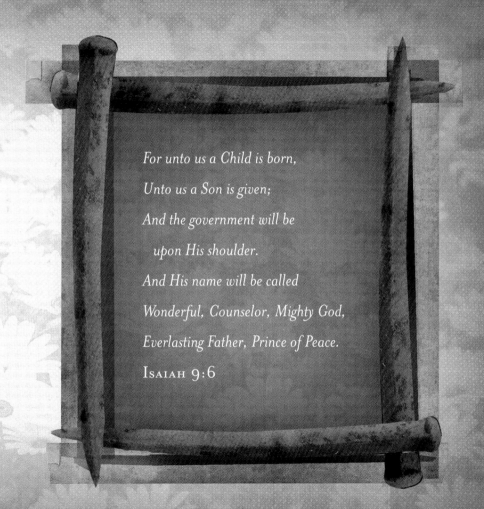

For unto us a Child is born,

Unto us a Son is given;

And the government will be

* upon His shoulder.*

And His name will be called

Wonderful, Counselor, Mighty God,

Everlasting Father, Prince of Peace.

Isaiah 9:6

47

Jesus the Christ extended

Mercy to the sinner

Compassion to the broken

Healing to the sick

Dignity to the outcast

Rest for the tired

Water for the thirsty

Food for the hungry

Strength for the weary

Hope for the hopeless

Freedom for the bound

He was wounded for our transgressions,
He was bruised for our iniquities;
The chastisement of our peace was upon Him,
And by His stripes we are healed (Isaiah 53:5).

He was *loved*
He was *betrayed*
He was *beaten*

HE WAS CRUCIFIED
HE DIED
HE WAS BURIED

AND THEN ON THE THIRD DAY...

✳ ✳ ✳ ✳ ✳

...He Conquered Death!

✳ ✳ ✳ ✳ ✳

I know my redeemer, He lives
To take away my shame
And He lives forever, I'll proclaim
The payment of my sin
Was the precious life He gave
But now He's alive and
There's an empty grave

51

Then He said to them, "Thus it is written, and thus it was necessary for the Christ to suffer and to rise from the dead the third day, and that repentance and remission of sins should be preached in His name to all nations, beginning at Jerusalem. And you are witnesses of these things."

Luke 24:46-48

In all their affliction He was afflicted,

And the Angel of His Presence saved them;

In His love and in His pity He redeemed them;

And He bore them and carried them

All the days of old.

Isaiah 63:9

He Lives! ❀ ❀ ❀

Job doesn't need a kinsman-redeemer. He doesn't
need somebody in the physical to come and redeem
him. He needs the spiritual. He needs Christ. He
needs God Himself to get him out of what he was in.
And God Himself shows up and does that.

Ruth and Naomi need a physical redeemer, they
need somebody who can come and supply for them,
somebody who can establish shelter over their heads
for the rest of their lives. They need somebody who
can carry on the names of their dead husbands.
That's what they need, and that's what they are
given. Even though they go through despair, they go
through hardship, obviously they don't give up, they
continue even though they don't know what is going
to happen. And God works a miracle for them. He
works on Boaz's heart.

It really shows to me the sovereignty of God and how God will go wherever He needs to go. He takes the most unlikely people, the people who are ordinary and common, and those are the people through whom He chooses to do something extraordinary. Ruth is a special testament of how God sets the foolish things to confound the wise—He takes somebody who was not a part of His people and grafts her into the lineage of Christ. The same people that God grafted in was a sign of the same kind of people He would redeem later. And so we find ourselves as Gentiles along with Jews being able to be redeemed.

Job doesn't know at the beginning of his pain that in the end it is going to be better, but he speaks from hope: I know my Redeemer lives. One who's going to save me out of this, One who's going to heal me and in the last days is going to stand upon the earth.

*J*ob's example gives hope to people, just to be able to say that in the midst of what I'm going through, there's one thing I'm willing to stake my life on—I know my Redeemer lives, and because He lives, He's going to get me through this. And really, if the worst happens to me, I'm going to see my Redeemer face to face. We endure hardship, that's a given fact in this world—but our Redeemer is *alive*.

OUR REDEEMER LIVES!

Now when He had taken the scroll, the four living creatures and the twenty-four elders fell down before the Lamb, each having a harp, and golden bowls full of incense, which are the prayers of the saints. And they sang a new song, saying:

"You are worthy to take the scroll,
And to open its seals;
For You were slain,
And have redeemed us to God by Your blood
Out of every tribe and tongue and people and nation,
And have made us kings and priests to our God;
And we shall reign on the earth."

REVELATION 5:8-10

NICOLE C. MULLEN'S
song "Redeemer" first earned acclaim on her
self-titled album *Nicole C. Mullen*, from Word
Records, a division of Word Entertainment.
The album, like its author, is vivacious, joyful,
and relentlessly enthusiastic, while maintaining
an uncanny ability to speak with honesty and
vulnerability about life as it is. And about life
as it should be. Nicole's album *Talk About It* also
reflects her musical versatility—the ballads
segue to pop, then urban grooves, with the
common denominator being the lyrical theme:
talking to and calling on the Lord.